A Quick Guide to Emotional Intelligence

This guide to Emotional Intelligence is here to help you understand why it has become so important for anyone looking to improve their personal or professional lives when communicating, whether that's with yourself or others. Improving your EI will lead to better quality relationships with the people that matter in your life. EI explores the pattern of behaviours that we run, or patterns of behaviours that run us! Every conversation or interaction we have leaves our unique fingerprint with that person. Depending on how Emotionally Intelligent you are determines the impression you leave! The ideal situation is to leave a positive fingerprint. I've also included some compelling data at the end of this guide to support the case for developing Emotional Intelligence.

Jim Rees

Overview of the EI Model

The model that I'll be referring to throughout, is from JCA Global. There are a number of different frameworks, yet I continue to use this when working with leaders and their teams. It's the only EI questionnaire that measures Self Regard and Regard for Others which comes from Transactional Analysis and is still used globally by councillors and Psychotherapists to unpack and explain human behaviour.

The reason I believe this to be important is that the report allows you to explore at a much deeper level, the various patterns of behaviour we run as human beings. It also helps the understanding of why certain behaviours have come about in our lives.

In total the JCA model measures 16 different scales, for which the core framework is below.

	Personal Intelligence	Interpersonal Intelligence
Behaviour	Self Management	Relationship Management
Feeling	Self Awareness	Awareness of Others
Attitude	Self Regard	Regard for Others

When looking at the core framework, it's obvious that one side of the scale measures Self or Personal Intelligence and the other side measures how you are with Others or Interpersonal Intelligence.

At the Attitude or foundation level of Emotional Intelligence are the scales of Self Regard and Regard for Others. These two scales are where it all starts and they are strongly interconnected throughout the model.

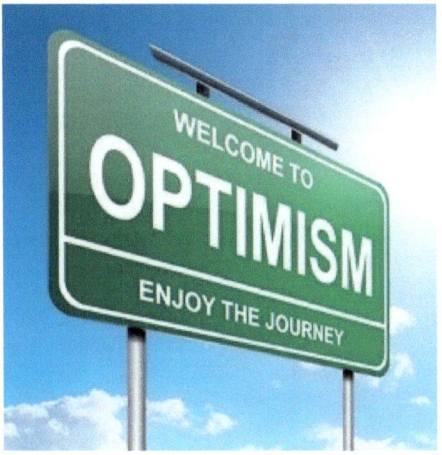

Self Regard

This scale is one of the most important aspects within Emotional Intelligence (EI). Your Self Regard is developed very early in life, some studies suggest as early 9 months onwards. As a young baby, the only way we can communicate is to cry out when we want something, whether it's to be picked up or we might be hungry, cold, too hot etc. Each time we cry out and the result is that we get picked up, we referred to this in Transactional Analysis as a positive stroke. If we are left to cry and not picked up, that would be a negative stroke!

So really what I'm talking about here is our conditioning, and that of course continues throughout our lifetime e.g. as a toddler starts to learn to walk they will be encouraged and praised as he or she continues to go from crawling to walking, their parents will clap and verbally praise their child, that's how we all learnt to walk! More positive strokes!

If you're lucky, your parents will have continued to reinforce the positive strokes by giving you a cuddle and then praising you for reading well or doing well in a test at school. There are lots of opportunities for parents to continue to add to the positive strokes as you grow up into being an adult.

It's very easy to see how a child grows up having a high Self Regard, which basically means that they are very comfortable in their skin, they are confident in their abilities and are usually happy to step up and try new things and meet new people in a confident way.

Self Regard Continued....

You can also see, if a child has missed out on a getting a lot of positive strokes when they were growing up, the impact this could have on their Self Regard e.g. a child constantly left to cry and without many positive strokes will likely end up with a lower Self Regard.

Take this to the extreme, picture a child growing up in an environment where all they ever got was negative strokes. They might have been smacked when they cried, they might not have got the cuddles or praise from either of their parents when they did well, in fact, they may have been told that they were useless and wouldn't amount to much in life!

Here you can quickly see how Self Regard is shaped. By the way, this is not meant to be a witch hunt to blame your parents, this is more about helping you understand how Self Regard is formed throughout your life.

Your Self Regard continues to be shaped as an adult via your friends and work colleagues, or not, as the case may be e.g. if you have a boss who doesn't really praise their team for the good work they do, that has the potential to erode your Self Regard.

People who score low on Self Regard tend to be their own worst critic, their internal dialog reinforces a low opinion of themselves and thus keeps them stuck with a low level of self confidence. This scale really is so important in being able to be happy and comfortable with yourself, the point being that you need to be able to love yourself first for you, to then be able to love others.

The good news is that all of us are capable of change. These aspects of you as a human being are not hard wired and even though you may have had a lifetime of conditioning, you can start the process of building a healthier Self Regard over time. All of the latest data around Neuroscience backs this up and new findings are being published on a regular basis.

By raising your awareness of your thinking patterns, which influence your behaviours and eventually become habits, you can change the story you've been telling yourself of who you are and then deliberately create a new, more confident and more fulfilled version of yourself.

It's worth pointing out that someone who scores high in Self Regard, won't necessarily mean they are self centred or arrogant, it just means that they are OK with themselves and they don't give themselves a hard time if they don't get something right the first time of asking.

Regard for Others

This scale is also shaped mainly by our parents. Around the age of 2-3 years we are starting to get a better understanding of language and we are observing how our parents interact with other people, how your Mum & Dad speak to your neighbours and everyone else they interact with. Even when they watch the TV and any comments they have will in turn be influencing you as you grow up. How they treat your siblings and any other relatives will all add to your view of how you should treat other people.

Regards for Others doesn't mean you have to agree with someone else's opinion or world view, it's more about valuing their opinion and whether you care for other people. From a Transactional Analysis point of view this is where the OK Corral comes from. Let me explain, having a high Self Regard = I'm OK, having a high Regard for Others = You're Ok.
These two positions are often referred to as your life positions, because they are formed early in life and usually stay with you throughout your life unless you become aware of your score and then deliberately work on yourself to enhance your scores.

The ideal life position is I'm OK, You're Ok and having an equal score for both scales is important. Measuring this on a scale of 1-10, the ideal score would be 10 & 10 for both scales, but in the thousands of executives I've worked with over the past 14 years, I have rarely seen someone score high on both scales.

As I mentioned earlier, these two scales of Self Regard & Regard for Others interlink with the rest of the scales and it's critical to fully understand the dynamic of how these two scales can play out in how they show up in your behaviour throughout your life. They are like a set of glasses, in terms of how you view and interact with yourself and others.

If you have a high Self Regard and a low Regard for Others, it would mean that you may be more interested in your own opinion and not really pay attention when someone else is attempting to share their view. You might also find it difficult to trust others, and perhaps believe that they wouldn't be able to complete a task in the same way you would approach it, and that they certainly wouldn't be as polished as yourself with the end result.

Regard for Others Continued....

If you had a low Self Regard and a high Regard for Others, that would play out very differently. This life position could lead to you being more concerned about other people's opinions by constantly asking what their view of the project or task is and doubting that you have much to offer the group you might be working with. You will also put other peoples needs before your own and will take the blame if something goes wrong within a team situation. If you are the boss of the team you'll end up protecting the team and taking responsibility, even if it's not your fault.

Having an equal balance of both of these scales is important for many reasons apart from the ones above, I have worked with a lot of very successful people who do have a low Self Regard and all of them have struggled with feeling good about themselves or believing that they are successful, even when the evidence and their results prove otherwise.

The most important relationship is the one you have with yourself. A low Self Regard can mean that you are constantly putting yourself down with negative self talk and you can get stuck in this pattern of not feeling good about yourself, which in turn, reinforces your negative thinking or worrying about your short comings.

Just knowing what your life positions are can have a big impact on your awareness, which can then become a catalyst for change, especially if you have the knowledge of what steps you can take to grow.

The OK Corral

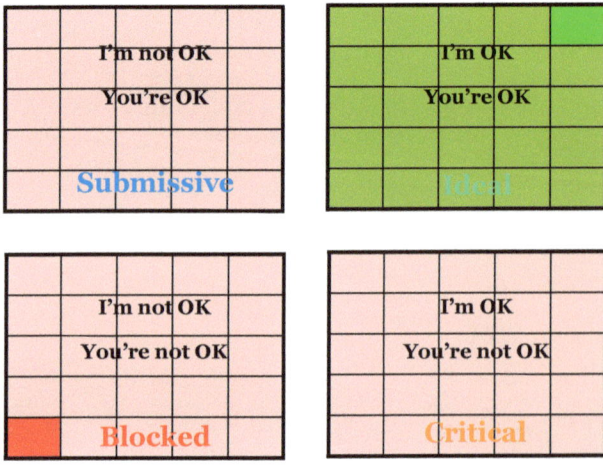

Self Awareness

Self Awareness is the corner stone to understanding and knowing yourself. This scale measures how in touch you are with yourself - do you notice how you are feeling and any subtle changes that you have in your physiology as you go about your daily activities? Are you aware of what impact your feelings have on your thinking and your behaviours as you interact with others in each moment throughout your busy schedule?

People who score well on Self Awareness pick up on when they are hungry or thirsty, they pay attention to the signals their body sends them and are usually very present and aware
of how they are being with other people when in a meeting. These individuals would rarely get distracted with their mobile phone whilst in a meeting as they would be conscious of the potential impact that it would have on other people, so they would turn it off or put it on silent so it didn't interrupt!

Someone who scores high here would also know how important their posture is and the relationship that it plays with their thinking and in turn how they behave.

A low score on Self Awareness will mean that a person will almost be sleep walking through their life and unaware of how they are showing up and the finger print they are leaving in all of the interactions they have with themselves and other people. They will likely skip lunch as they will pay little attention to the bodies signals, as they can get self absorbed whilst working on a project.

Awareness of Others

Some people who score low on Regard for Others are often surprised and mistake it with Awareness for Others which is very different. Many leaders believe that it is their job to be aware of other peoples behaviours which will mean that their teams are constantly being observed and judged.

A high Awareness of Others should ideally be linked with a high Regard for Others which means that the leader actually cares about their team member, and their awareness of others is as a result of them being genuinely interested in the other person. This is very different from someone thinking that it's their job to judge and catch people out who might have a low Regard for Others, so even though they may have a high Awareness of Others score, it will be driven from a place of not really caring about the other person's view or opinion and can be due to a low level of trust.

Typically, when someone is low on this scale they will miss the subtle signs of when someone else might be stressed or not happy with the way a discussion is going within a team setting e.g. the verbal and non verbal signals that people give off will be missed or mis-interpreted.

If someone has a high score for Self Awareness, they will be able to develop their Awareness for Others, as they will have become good at noticing the subtle changes within themselves and be more conscious of what to look for in others.

The Self Management Scales

The following aspects of your Emotional Intelligence all look at how well you manage yourself. These are the tools that you go to when you are handling the various situations that show up throughout your day. It's rare to see someone score high in every aspect of these scales, usually 2-3 are favoured and are used or sometimes over used when you are responding to the events that show up.

I have already written about Self Awareness separately and want to reinforce the importance that it plays in everything we do, that's why I believe it's good to go and seek feedback from everyone that you interact with regularly. Your family will do this naturally and there's a lot we can learn, as they are closest to us and know us well!

The biggest first step we can take in improving ourselves is to heighten our Self Awareness. The next step is to then do something with this new level of awareness, even a slight change can bring about remarkable results.

Emotional Resilience

In todays busyness, being Emotionally Resilient has become a must have in your tool kit for being able to handle yourself and keep a level head amongst all of the bombardment that can take place during a typical day.

Emotional Resilience Continued....

This is about being able to deal with juggling your usual duties whilst managing minor setbacks that show up throughout your day e.g. being delayed on your journey into work can raise the stress levels, especially if it means that you are now under even more pressure to get a proposal competed on time.

Whether it's a minor setback or a big hole you've just encountered, being able to pick yourself up and dust yourself off so you can carry on is a major attribute to have up your sleeve. This becomes a real issue if you get derailed by one of these speed bumps and it
can chip away at your resilience causing you to become unable to handle the next little bump that shows up in your day, all of a sudden you can spiral out of control if this is not kept in check. The old classic saying of:- the straw that broke the camels back springs to mind here, where, if your Emotional Resilience (ER) is low, it can be the tinniest of things that can ruin your day!

World class athletes on the whole have high levels of ER and are able to perform under enormous stress to be able to achieve their goals. There is a simple model that they use when handling any unexpected curve balls, this is :- E+R=O Experience + Response = Outcome. Most of the time we have very little control over the Experience, things like weather, traffic, rude people, the economy, someone scratching your car whilst it's parked at the shops, there's a huge list of things that just happen. How we Respond to those Experiences is on the whole in our control. Some people would argue that they can't help how they respond to certain things in life but peak performers own how they react to each Experience or situation, they take 100% personal responsibility for how they behave.

Typically, what happens is, we have an Experience or event happen, and then almost immediately, we react. Sometimes it's just a knee jerk response, and we don't even think about it! Highly successful athletes and leaders alike are able to stay focused in these situations and concentrate on the Outcome that they want. So in the future when an Experience catches you out, stay focused on your desired Outcome and then choose the most appropriate response to get your desired Outcome.

This model is in play from the moment we wake up in the morning until we go back to sleep at night and can transform your life if you can stay aware of what your desired Outcome is when the curve balls are thrown in life.

Personal Power

Having high Personal Power means that you take a high level of personal responsibility for the outcomes or results that are showing up for you in your life. If you score low here, it could be that you feel that life is just happening to you and you feel you have little or no control of how your life is turning out.

Someone scoring low here could suggest that they are focusing on everything else apart from themselves, they could blame the economy, the government, their parents, their schooling or lack of education, it could be that they were an only child or one of 6 or 7 children and they blame this for how they've turned out in life. There are so many reasons why they won't take personal responsibility.

If someone scores low on Self Regard, usually their Emotional Resilience and Personal Power are lowered as well. These individuals have been worn down by their lives and the results they have been getting and can get caught in a trap of thinking whatever they do, it's not going to change things by much! There is an energy that goes with these people, they expect the worst and hope for the best, but in truth, they're not expecting much from life.

On the other hand, someone who scores high on this scale, is someone who also has high Self Awareness and also scores high on Reflective Learning, as they are constantly on the lookout to improve themselves by asking others for feedback. They also take 100% personal responsibility for the results that they get in their lives.

Goal Directedness

With the Self Management scales, I usually see one or two that stand out as high scores. We can get so used to using one of the scales that it stops us from developing the other aspects of our self management tools.

This scale of Goal Directedness is one of the scales that a lot of people do tend to fall back on and can rely too heavily upon, for example, someone might score low on their Emotional Resilience and have low Personal Power but over compensates by using their high Goal Directedness to get things done and push a project through by staying focused on the goal.

This is all about whether your behaviours match your long term goals. It could be that you get easily distracted and stray away from staying focused on getting the tasks done that align to your goals.

If you score low here, it could be that you have a higher Regard for Others and you drop your own goals to support others to achieve their goals. People who score high here are the sort of people who set out their goals and then do whatever it takes to complete them, sometimes this can be to the point of being a little obsessed.

Flexibility

Being flexible is a great attribute to have, it means you are able to consider different people's views and opinions and then navigate a more emotionally intelligent conversation. People who score low on this scale can struggle to change their thinking and their behaviours to an ever changing environment. Usually this is down to our conditioning that has happened as a young child growing up with a certain set of values and beliefs that have been embedded throughout their lifetime.

The saying "Don't talk to strangers" could prevent you from wanting to meet new people at a networking event. Other examples of a low Flexibility score are:- having fixed routines for doing certain tasks, taking the same route in your car, not being able to pick up the phone and make a call to book an appointment, not wanting to try a new way of doing something, or eating a new food dish, sleeping the same side of the bed.

Individuals who score high here are usually happy to jump straight into new situations and explore what works for them. They are also happy to ask other people their opinions to see if there is a better way to complete a task that they are looking to finish. They are also mindful of taking the time to think about other potential options and how they might engage in conversations.

Connecting with Others

How good are you at making new connections with other people? Is this something you find easy to do, or do you avoid this completely? This can be at a party where you're meeting people for the first time or it could be a networking meeting and you have to introduce yourself and make small talk.

People who have a high Self Regard combined with a high Regard for Others will find this fairly easy to do. These are people who are comfortable in their own skin and also care about other people as well.

If you have a low Self Regard, you may feel that you lack the self confidence to be able to introduce yourself within a new group and you might go out of your way to avoid these situations - sometimes career choices are made so that individuals don't have to interact with other people. A sales person for example, requires the ability to effortlessly connect with others, it will be a core attribute for them and will encourage others to in turn, be more open.

I'm sure you will have been in situations where you feel as though you are the one doing all of the talking, this could just be down to the fact, that the person you're speaking with is shy and finds it hard to make those connections.

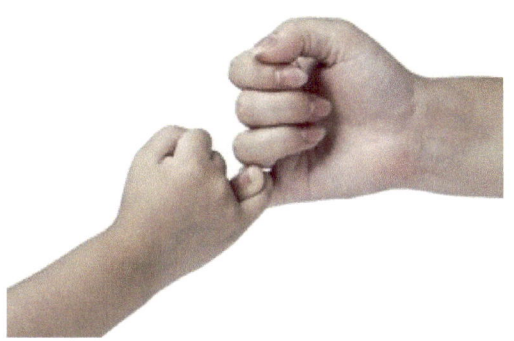

Authenticity

This scale measures whether you not only "talk the talk" but you also "walk the walk", what it suggests is whether you follow through on commitments that you make to others and whether what you say is the same as what you do as a person.

Some classic examples of low Authenticity would be someone suggesting that being fit and healthy is really important to themselves and yet they are overweight and have a really poor diet, or that it's important to be on time but they are always late. Also, leaders who talk about making sure that the company value of having a work life balance is important but then send e-mails out late at night or over the weekend, will also give off the wrong message to their teams.

A lack of Authenticity can be picked up fairly quickly by most people, so this scale is an important one to have if you want to develop strong relationships. If you let people down, that will then in turn compromise their trust in you. If you have little trust in someone it will take time before you can develop enough good experiences of them to have a proper connection.

The Relationship Management Scales

The following scales look at how you manage yourself when interacting with others. Being a highly Emotionally Intelligent person requires you to score well on the Personal and Interpersonal aspects of EI. There are certain jobs that require you to be able to maintain healthy relationships e.g. if you lead a team or if you are constantly meeting new people within your role representing your company. The ability to be flexible when interacting with others can give you such a competitive edge and is seen more and more now as a game changer in most organisations.

All of the scales within the relationship management Report that I use from JCA global are scored using a bipolar measurement system. This means that there are three scales in each of the following aspects that we will be looking at.

As an example, the first scale that we are looking at, is that of trust, the ideal situation is to score well on the middle scale of carefully trusting and the outlying scales of mis- trusting and over trusting to score low.

11. Trust:

A. Mistrustful: (2.5000)
B. Carefully trusting: (4.2500)
C. Over trusting: (4.0000)

Trust

Trust is an interesting one within relationships, the goal within relationships being carefully trusting. Depending on your upbringing and how your parents interacted with others, it's possible for you to be mistrustful of other people, it's also the case that you could be over trusting if your parents were very open and highly trusting with others.

If you're mistrustful as a leader, this may have an impact on how much you delegate to your team. On the other hand, if you are over trusting this could mean that you give too much responsibility to your team members without checking their capability levels, as to whether they can do the task or not.

Both aspects of being either mistrustful or over trusting can have a major impact on the relationship that you are trying to develop. Having the ability to be carefully trusting is about asking great questions and getting to know each individual within your team and their unique set of capabilities. Without trust you will struggle to build a strong team.

Balanced Outlook

The three scales of balanced outlook are pessimistic, realistically optimistic and over optimistic. You can very quickly see the difference each of the outlying scales can have on how you view world and the different outcomes being pessimistic or over optimistic can have when you're trying to achieve a goal.

There is a difference between critical thinking and being pessimistic. The pessimist tends to be very good at seeing fault within a plan, which of course can be a good thing but the challenge is that the pessimist can get stuck in this negative pattern of thinking and struggle to come up with solutions. Critical thinking is all about thinking through the potential things that might go wrong and then coming up with a strategy to cover these possibilities.

You can also see if you were being over optimistic how this may trip you up. Someone who has the thought that everything will all be okay has the potential to miss the glaringly obvious speed bumps that might show up within a project. The same is true when thinking about relationships with other people - it's very easy for someone who is over optimistic to end up trusting someone that they've only just met.

So the way to grow your realistically optimistic scale is to use critical thinking to your advantage and at the same time look for more data or evidence to prevent you from being over optimistic.

Emotional Expression and Control

As with all of these scales, emotional expression and control will have been shaped and conditioned predominantly throughout your childhood via your parents and teachers and other close family members. As a young child growing up you will have sat around the family table and experienced how your parents handled any potential arguments as a couple.

When you disagree with somebody or they have a different view, it's important to be able to stay free and in charge of your emotions. How your parents settled their disagreements will have shaped how you handle your emotions when interacting with other people. For example, when an argument started with your parents, it could have ended up in a shouting match, if that were the case in your household, both of your parents will have been under controlled (they have the potential to flip out).

The other end of the spectrum is when one or both parents are over controlled. This basically means that they bottle things up and don't discuss them with anyone. These individuals can be really tough to read and a lot of the time you're not sure where you stand with them.

I can certainly remember the leaders that I have worked with, who were very under controlled and most of the time myself and the rest of the team would be walking on egg shells, and had to check to make sure that the boss was in a good mood before we approached them.

Someone who scores highly on being free and in charge is typically a great listener and has the ability to see everyone's perspective. They are also able to calmly express themselves even if the debate gets heated.

Conflict Handling

As a leader, being able to handle conflict is critical. The big challenge for most of us is being able to get the balance right between passive and aggressive behaviours. The goal when handling conflict is to remain assertive, you certainly don't want to be too passive and just rollover but at the same time you need to keep any aggression in check so that you don't scare the other individual.

As with the previous scale of emotional expression and control, conflict handling requires you to be free and in charge of your emotions, so the goal in conflict handling is to remain focused on the outcome that you want and to remain calm at all times. One of the best tips I've learnt over the years is to spend some time before the meeting to think things through from the other persons perspective, or in other words, walk a mile in their shoes.

Attempting to understand what the other person might be thinking and feeling from their perspective is a really good use of your time. Thinking about the words that they might use to describe you as their leader and what they might say about how you've handled this situation, might uncover some useful insights. Another suggestion would be to see things from the third persons point of view (as a fly on the wall), again this can uncover aspects of the conflict that you might not have considered.

When there's a lot at stake and emotions are running high the brains typical response is that of fight, flight or freeze and typically a heated conversation can either become violent or will go silent - these are the two extreme ends of where you want the conversation to be.
The ideal goal is to end up with a shared understanding and an agreed way of working together moving forward.

Interdependence

Getting the right balance between being dependent on other peoples opinions when making a decision, or being overly independent and not seeking out anyone else's views, usually links back to your Self Regard and your Regard for Others. If you have a high Self Regard and a low Regard for Others this could mean that you end up with high over independent score.

The reverse is also the case, if you have a low Self Regard and a high Regard for Others, this can play out with you relying too heavily on seeking out other peoples opinions and you can self-doubt whether you're own view has anything to add, for you to then be able make an informed decision.

Scoring high on the Interdependence scale also requires a high level of Flexibility and if you are overly independent it's worth spending time getting feedback from your team and others about how they feel when you're working with them on a project. You will also benefit from feedback if you score highly on being Dependant.

Reflective Learning

Within organisations, Reflective Learning has become a big blindspot. The pace of working has continued to increase year on year with same time emails, text messages and conference calls. Add to this, the pressure of staying ahead of your competitors and the speed of getting back to your clients has eroded the time to sit and reflect.

The expectation of the corporate treadmill is that clients expect quick responses to any enquiries or request for proposals and there is a certain pace that companies have become addicted to, causing increased pressure and stress for the individuals within the organisations.

As much as I would agree with the idea of not being able to drive your car forward by looking backwards, I don't believe the pace of next next next is healthy for the long-term growth of an organisation. Time must be set aside to review how last month or the last quarter has played out for you and your team, a simple framework of Win Learn Change can be applied when looking back at your performance.

Ask these three simple questions:-

What worked well?
So the focus here when reflecting, is all about the good stuff that happened, even if you're looking at a situation where you didn't get the result that you wanted.

What did I/We Learn?
This is fairly obvious and invites you to look at what you have learnt from the process.

Reflective Learning Continued....

What do I/we need to change?
It may be that you don't need to change anything, or it could uncover that
you need to increase your activities in certain steps of the process.

This is such an Achilles heel in large global organisations where silos have
evolved over time, the main cause being that they don't communicate with
each other and share the learning from the different divisions within the
organisation. I believe this aspect of being able to have cross functional
reflective learning sessions would give companies a significant competitive
edge.

The Case for Developing Emotional Intelligence

For many years organisations have grappled with the idea of whether there
was a case for spending time and more importantly, money on developing
what was often called the 'Soft Skills' within the company. In the past 10
years more and more data points have been pulled together which
overwhelming prove the role and the importance Emotional Intelligence
plays in being able to maintain a competitive advantage in an ever changing
and dynamic marketplace.

The Case for Developing Emotional Intelligence Continued....

Just looking at the below graph from Zenger & Folkman's research, shows that having the Technical skills and a high level of Motivation are not enough to be an Exceptional Leader, you **must** have the Emotional quotient which is the bit that is the 'difference that makes the difference' when looking at 20,000 Leaders in their research. In other words, you can have two competing leaders from different companies who have the same level of technical skills and are equally motivated, but it's the one who has a higher level of Emotional Intelligence who has the ability to interact more effectively with their clients and their team/peers who will win the day.

Technical Quotient	Motivation Quotient	Emotional Quotient	Exceptional
Strength	Not a strength	Not a strength	0%
Not a strength	Strength	Not a strength	0.5%
Not a strength	Not a strength	Strength	1.4%
Strength	Strength	Strength	87%

Zenger & Folkman, 'The Extraordinary Leader', 200,000 assessments on 20,000 leaders

Above is Gallup's Global Engagement research, which is another compelling piece of information that points to the importance of getting the Hearts & Minds aligned organisationally.

The Case for Developing Emotional Intelligence Continued....

The last data point taken in 2013 shows little improvement from the 2010 figures and I believe this is a current Blindspot in the corporate market. When all is said and done over a billion people were studied, and a staggering 24% were disengaged, 63% of staff were not motivated, leaving only 13% of people who were fully engaged.

Internal company surveys don't always uncover the Truth of what's going on, as most people feel vulnerable that the survey is not confidential, this in itself causes an unclear message back to the leaders who are attempting to get a temperature check on where the company is at a given point in time.

A large majority of the aspects that would help improve people being more engaged, are linked very closely to EI e.g. things like Self Awareness, Awareness of Others, Regard for Others, Trust, Conflict Handling, Connecting with Others and having the ability for leaders to be more coach-like in their approach all require a high EI score.

In another study, Rosier looked at 181 different positions from 121 organisations worldwide and found that **67%** of the abilities deemed essential for effective performance, were Emotional Competencies.

AT&T found that **91%** of their top performers were high in Emotional Intelligence.

At Siemens, senior managers trained in Emotional Intelligence delivered an additional **$1.5** million profit, double the comparison group that had no such training.

Although this is not a comprehensive list of all of the data, I hope it's enough to convince you the reader that developing Emotional Intelligence within your organisations will yield a return on your investment.

Finally, as a business, we focus on Executive Coaching, Leadership Alignment and Building World Class Teams.

Contact us at jim@jimrees.co.uk for further information or to organise an exploratory meeting.

Our website is www.thelongandtheshortofit.biz

www.ingramcontent.com/pod-product-compliance
Lightning Source LLC
Chambersburg PA
CBHW040328010626

45792CB00024B/2315